Luke's Flute

By Carmel Reilly

Luke jumped for joy.

He would play his flute
in the school band!

Luke ran home to tell Nan.

"That is great!" said Nan.

"But I'm a bit scared,"
Luke said.

"Why?" said Nan.

"The school band is such
a big deal," said Luke.
"What if my flute playing
is not all right?"

"You play so well!" said Nan.

"But it's hard to play for other kids, Nan," said Luke. "Do you get what I mean?"

"Yes, I do," said Nan.
"I had to sing a tune
for other kids once."

"I had a bad dream that
I could not sing," said Nan.
"I was in my cute dress,
and I forgot the tune!"

"That **is** a bad dream!"
said Luke.
"What if I get up there
and forget the tune?"

"It will be all right, Luke,"
said Nan.
"On the day, I sang very well."

"I'm still scared," said Luke.
"What if the other kids are rude?"

"They will not be rude!"
said Nan.
"The best thing to do
is train hard."

Luke trained hard on his flute
for weeks.

At last, it was time to play
with the school band.

Nan came to see Luke play.

Luke was not scared
any more.

If Nan could sing for other kids,
he could play his flute!

Luke played his flute very well!

CHECKING FOR MEANING

1. Why was Luke a bit scared to play his flute in the school band? *(Literal)*

2. Why did Nan understand how Luke was feeling? *(Literal)*

3. What was Nan's advice to Luke? *(Inferential)*

EXTENDING VOCABULARY

flute	Make a list of words that describe a flute, e.g. long, thin, light, shiny.
tune	What is another name for a *tune*? E.g. song. What is your favourite tune?
rude	What does it mean to be *rude*? What are other words that have a similar meaning? E.g. bad mannered, cheeky.

MOVING BEYOND THE TEXT

1. If you were in the school band, which instrument would you like to play? Why?

2. Has someone in your family given you some good advice? What was it? Did you try to do what they said? How successful were you?

3. Why do some people become nervous when they have to perform for other people? How does your body react when you get nervous?

4. What did Luke do to make sure he could play his flute well? What things do you do that need a lot of practice?

SPEED SOUNDS

oo	ue	ew	ui	u_e
ou	u	oe	o	

PRACTICE WORDS

flute

Luke

you

to

do

Do

cute

tune

rude